Building **S**kills in **W**riting

Responding to Literature

BY KAREN KELLAHER

SCHOLASTIC
PROFESSIONAL **B**OOKS

NEW YORK • TORONTO • LONDON • AUCKLAND • SYDNEY
MEXICO CITY • NEW DELHI • HONG KONG • BUENOS AIRES

To Mom,

with thanks for all your love

and support

Front cover and interior design by Kathy Massaro
Cover art by Jon Buller
Interior art by Michael Moran
Poster art by Laura Cornell

ISBN: 0-439-28841-X
Copyright © 2002 by Karen Kellaher
Published by Scholastic Inc.
All rights reserved.
Printed in the U.S.A.

1 2 3 4 5 6 7 8 9 10   40   09 08 07 06 05 04 03 02

Contents

Introduction 4
   About This Series 4
   About This Book 4
   Correlations With the Language Arts Standards 5
   Teaching With the Poster:
     Recipe for Good Writing—
     Juicy Book Reviews 5

CHAPTER 1

Getting Started: Selecting Literature 7
* Four Criteria to Consider........................ 7
The Write Stuff:
   Profiles of Recommended Books.......... 10
   TEACHER CHECKLIST: Does This Book
     Model Traits of Effective Writing? 12

CHAPTER 2

The ABC's of Response Journals 14
* Introducing Dialogue Journals
   to Your Classroom 15
What to Expect From Student Entries—
   And How to Respond 16
Tracking Your Journal Rotation 20
Side Trips: Other Types of Journaling 20
   * Buddy Journal 20
   * Predict-and-Check Journal 20
   "Virtual Reality" Journal 21
   * Prompt-a-Day Idea Cube 21
   TEACHER RUBRIC: How Well Are My Students
     Responding to Literature? 26
   TEACHER CHECKLIST: Tracking Your Journal
     Rotation 27

CHAPTER 3

**Other Creative Ways
to Respond to Literature**................. 28

   It's a Cover-Up! (Creating Book Jackets)
   Writing Skills: Summarizing
     and Identifying Main Ideas 28

* **Character Cards**
   Writing Skills: Exploring Character 30
* **Book Talk—A Literature Talk Show**
   Writing Skills: Exploring Plot, Character,
     and Dialogue 32
Don't Let It End This Way!
   Writing Skills: Writing New Endings
     and Sequels 34
Plot-Pattern Puzzle
   Writing Skills: Exploring Plot Patterns.......... 36
* **Scene-Setting Travel Brochure**
   Writing Skills: Exploring Setting 37
What's the Word?
(Creating Text for Wordless Books)
   Writing Skills: Exploring Plot, Character,
     and Dialogue 41
* **Plot Pop-Up Book**
   Writing Skills: Exploring Story Beginnings,
     Middles, and Endings....................... 42
Dear Author… (Writing to Favorite Authors)
   Writing Skills: Advancing Judgments
     and Questions About Literature 45
* **Story-Spinner Wheel**
   Writing Skills: Exploring Story Elements 47
* **Main Idea Sun**
   Writing Skills: Responding to Nonfiction 50

CHAPTER 4

**Wrapping Up Literature-Response
Projects: Suggestions for Editing,
Publishing, and Assessing** 52

   STUDENT CHECKLIST:
     Editing My Own Work 54
   STUDENT CHECKLIST: Editing Symbols 55
   TEACHER RUBRIC: Assessing Student
     Literature Response 56

* INCLUDES REPRODUCIBLE KIDS' PAGE(S)

Introduction

ABOUT THIS SERIES:
Building Skills in Writing

Most of us write every day. We write when we make a grocery list, when we e-mail a faraway friend, and when we prepare our lesson plans. But rarely do we stop to think about what we're really doing when we put pen to paper or fingers to keyboard. What, exactly, is writing?

Educator Donald Murray once said that writing is the act of using language to "discover meaning in experience and communicate it."* For me, this definition sums up the most important aspects of the writing process. First, it reminds us that writing is rooted in personal experience. Without experience, we have no meaning to communicate. Second, Murray's definition underscores the fact that writing always has a purpose and an audience. The very idea of "communicating" meaning implies that there is someone to receive the message, even if that audience is simply oneself at a later moment in time.

As teachers of emergent writers, you have an exciting job—to help bring this definition to life for your students. This series, *Building Skills in Writing*, is designed to assist you in this role. Each of the three books—*Responding to Literature*, *Story Writing*, and *Report Writing*—features lessons, strategies, activities, reproducibles, teaching tips, rubrics, and checklists to help your students write for a specific purpose and audience. Each addresses all stages of the writing process, from prewriting through publishing and assessment.

ABOUT THIS BOOK:
Responding to Literature

The processes of reading and writing are as closely linked as those of speaking and listening. Therefore it makes sense to make responding to quality literature a cornerstone of your writing curriculum. In writing book reviews, character sketches, journal entries, sequels, and other responses to literature, children enter into a story more completely. They tend to construct deeper meaning from the text than if they had simply finished the book and walked away. Responding to literature is also a great way to explore the various genres of writing available to us. For example, one student might write a letter to the editor of her local newspaper after reading a nonfiction book about air pollution. Another might write a personal narrative about the death of a pet after being touched by a similar story.

Learning by Teaching: Selected Articles on Writing and Teaching. Upper Montclair, New Jersey: Boynton/Cook, 1982, p. 10

Another reason to have students write responses to literature is that good books model effective writing techniques, such as catchy beginnings, punchy dialogue, and logical organization. By inviting your students to read and respond to such books, you're encouraging them to incorporate those same techniques into their own writing.

In this book you'll find lessons, strategies, and activities to help you get students started in responding to literature. Specifically, the book will help you teach students to:

◎ summarize the text and focus on its key elements.

◎ organize the text by taking notes and making webs and other graphic organizers.

◎ advance judgments about the text.

◎ support judgments with references to the text itself, other works, and personal knowledge and experience.

◎ edit for grammar, punctuation, spelling, and capitalization.

◎ present literature response in interesting and creative formats.

◎ evaluate their own and others' literature response.

TEACHING WITH THE POSTER:
Recipe for Good Writing— Juicy Book Reviews

This book includes a pullout poster on writing an effective book review. I chose a recipe theme for the poster because I love to cook almost as much as I love to write—and I have found a surprising number of similarities between the two activities. In both cooking and writing, the creator follows a set of guidelines but still has a lot of room for creative personal touches. In both activities, the enjoyment comes not only from a delightful finished product but also from the work itself.

Display the poster and refer to it frequently as students write book reviews. Distribute smaller copies of the poster for students to color and use as learning place mats (see page 7). Students can tape the mini-posters to their desks or insert them in binders for homework help. For best results, laminate the place mats or glue them onto sheets of construction paper. As students prepare to write their own book reviews, show some examples of reviews in *Booklist* and other magazines.

Correlations With the Language Arts Standards

The activities in this book are aligned with the following language arts standards outlined by the Mid-Continent Regional Educational Laboratory (MCREL), an organization that collects and synthesizes noteworthy national and state K–12 curriculum standards.

◎ Writes in response to literature:

● summarizes main ideas and important details

● relates own ideas to supporting details

● advances judgments with references to the text and personal knowledge

◎ Uses prewriting strategies such as graphic organizers and note-taking to plan written work

◎ Uses strategies to draft, organize, and revise written work

◎ Uses strategies to edit and publish written work

◎ Evaluates own and others' writing

Source: *A Compendium of Standards and Benchmarks for K–12 Education* (Mid-Continent Regional Educational Laboratory, 1995).

Juicy Book Reviews

Recipe for Good Writing

Ingredients:
- ◎ **Book title**
- ◎ **Author**
- ◎ **Summary**
- ◎ **Opinion**
- ◎ **Details to support opinion**

Directions:

1 Pick a rich, flavorful book. You can use any variety—fiction, nonfiction, poetry, chapter books, or picture books.

2 Savor the book. Think about your favorite parts.

3 Sprinkle the **book title** and **author** on the page.

4 Stir in a **summary** of the book. A summary tells what the book is mainly about. Make sure you don't give away the ending!

5 Add a dash of your **opinion**. Describe what you liked or did not like about the book. Tell whether you think others would enjoy the book.

6 Top off your review with **details** or examples from the book that support your opinion.

7 Before serving, remove any mistakes in grammar and spelling. Ask a partner to "taste" your book review and help you find ways to "spice it up."

Serving Suggestion:

Trade book reviews with your classmates. Their reviews will help you choose a new book to read!

SCHOLASTIC

ILLUSTRATION BY LAURA CORNELL

Building Skills in Writing: Responding to Literature   Scholastic Professional Books

Getting Started: Selecting Literature

lmost any piece of literature can serve as a springboard for student response. You can use picture books, chapter books, nonfiction, poetry, magazine and newspaper articles, even content-area textbooks—anything that sparks interest and personal reflection among your students. To narrow your selection, consider the following specific criteria:

1 Does the literature reflect your students' special interests and concerns?

Not surprisingly, students respond most thoughtfully to topics near and dear to them. If you have a class full of animal lovers (and what second- or third-grade teacher doesn't!), try using an informative nonfiction title such as *The Magic School Bus: In the Time of the Dinosaurs* by Joanna Cole and Bruce Degen, or a warm and fuzzy tale such as Eric Carle's *The Very Hungry Caterpillar*. If your students are mad about monsters, invite them to read and respond to a mock scary story, such as Mike Thaler's *The Teacher From the Black Lagoon* or Maurice Sendak's classic *Where the Wild Things Are*.

Of course, your students' interests will be as unique as the students themselves. It is therefore ideal to let students choose their own material for literature response when possible. One technique is to select a number of books—one for every four to six students in your class—and let students sign up to read the book of their choice. Try to give each student his or her first or second choice. If you find that no one wants to read a particular title, consider changing it to something more appealing. Or, if it's a title you're convinced kids will love once they start reading, perform a two-minute "advertisement" for the book. Reveal just enough to whet children's appetites!

Once you've made book assignments, have each book group meet at least twice—once about halfway through the book and once after everyone has finished reading. Students should discuss favorite and least-favorite parts and characters, make and check predictions, and evaluate the book as a whole. This discussion will get students in gear for journal writing and other response activities (explored at greater length in chapters 2 and 3).

Is the literature at your students' reading level?

Few school experiences are as frustrating as trying to tackle a text that's well out of reach. Although we certainly want to challenge young readers, a text that forces a child to stop several times per sentence to look up a word meaning is probably too challenging. If you're not sure whether a title is appropriate for a given student, check readability by asking the student to read a page or passage aloud. (Do this quietly during individual conference time to respect students' privacy.) One tried-and-true rule of thumb is the "five-finger test." Here's how it works: As the student reads, have him raise one finger each time he encounters an unfamiliar word he cannot understand through context clues. If the student finds five such words on one page or in one passage, consider recommending that he save that particular text for later in the year. Then help him find a new book to respond to—preferably on the same topic or in the same genre. With some experience at this, your students will eventually be able to do the five-finger test independently; it's an easy way to gauge readability on their own.

By keeping readability in mind, you can help every child in your class feel like a successful reader and writer. Know, however, that readability is not the only factor in choosing literature—or even necessarily the most important one. Remember that students can often read above level if a topic is particularly interesting to them. There are also ways to compensate for a reading level that's slightly too high. For example, if you'd love the class to respond to a particular book but are concerned that the reading level may be too difficult, consider reading the book aloud either in one sitting or over a period of several days. Students often understand more from hearing a story read aloud than they do from reading it on their own.

 Does the literature reflect and respect different races, ethnicities, cultures, and genders?

Literature has the power to reflect and dignify human experience. Many of us— how lucky we are!—can remember at least one book that made us stop and say, "That's how I feel, too!" or "That character reminds me a lot of myself." As teachers of reading and writing, you can help *all* children find such a personal link with literature. How? When choosing literature for student response, look for books written by and about people of all races, ethnicities, and cultures. And be sure to make books available with both female and male central characters (by the third grade, many students seek out books revolving around characters of their own gender). Reading or hearing stories that reflect their own experiences can make children feel part of the larger human community. When children are *not exposed* to stories about people like themselves—or when they hear stories that paint thoughtless or negative stereotypes of their cultures—they may come to feel alienated from literature.

Obviously, reading about diverse cultures and experiences benefits everyone. One does not need to be Asian-American to be moved by Allen Say's immigration story, *Grandfather's Journey*. And a child who is not Jewish can still understand the miracle that occurs in Fran Manushkin's moving Hanukkah tale, *Latkes and Applesauce*. In fact, exposing all children to multicultural literature is simply paving the way for greater understanding and respect among diverse groups.

 Does the literature model the writing traits you want to teach?

If you expect students to dedicate time and effort to reading and responding to a book, the book itself ought to be of high caliber. Although it is difficult to pinpoint the precise characteristics of a high-quality book, there are some general attributes you can look for. When choosing fiction, look for a well-developed plot, setting, and characters. Make sure the book has vivid language and interesting dialogue. And trust your own judgment: Chances are, a book that you love to read with kids again and again is a good one.

When choosing nonfiction for literature response, stick with books that boast good organization, plenty of details and examples, and imagery that paints a picture of the topic. It's also important that you check for accuracy. Although it's not always easy to spot mistakes (especially when a topic is relatively new to you), you can do your best by comparing several works on the same subject and by reading reviews in publications such as *Booklist* and *Horn Book*. Look especially closely at books published a decade or more ago; although they may be perfectly up-to-date, there's also a chance the information has changed since the book was published, especially on technology-driven topics such as computers.

In addition to searching for general good quality, you may also wish to hunt for literature that exemplifies the specific writing traits you're teaching. For example, when you want to give students experience in writing catchy beginnings, have students read and respond to a story with a great start. When you're teaching dialogue, make sure your literature-response selection is chock-full of zippy conversation (try, for example, some of Marc Brown's *Arthur* titles). Seeing how professional authors master a technique can help motivate students and give a real-life context to your writing lessons.

The reproducible checklist on page 12 summarizes various criteria to consider when evaluating both fiction and nonfiction books for your students. The reproducible bookmark on page 13 includes tips for students to keep in mind when responding to the books they read.

Obviously, matching literature to specific writing traits is no easy task. You'll need to allow plenty of prep time to review books thoroughly—and you'll likely become a regular at your local children's library or bookstore! On index cards, keep track of the specific traits modeled in each book you read. The book list on the following two pages provides a model you can use.

The Write Stuff:
Profiles of Recommended Books

The following books will help you introduce second- and third-graders to some specific techniques of effective writing. Of course, these titles are merely a drop in the bucket; you'll find many more wonderful titles on your own.

─────── **FICTION** ───────

Abuela
by Arthur Dorros

SUMMARY: Rosalba and her abuela ("grandmother" in Spanish) go on an imaginary adventure in the clouds, where they see all kinds of shapes. Cloud shapes (cat, bear, and so on) are named in Spanish, so students get a taste of the language.

USE IT TO MODEL: Setting

Alexander and the Terrible, Horrible, No Good, Very Bad Day
by Judith Viorst

SUMMARY: Poor Alexander wakes up with chewing gum in his hair—and his day only gets worse!

USE IT TO MODEL: Great beginnings, character development, dialogue, action

Beezus and Ramona
by Beverly Cleary

SUMMARY: Beezus's patience is tested over and over by her mischievous four-year-old sister, Ramona.

USE IT TO MODEL: Character development, dialogue, and effective endings

The Day of Ahmed's Secret
by Florence Parry Heide

SUMMARY: Ahmed waits through a busy day to share a secret with his family and with readers: He has learned to write his name. Although the concept of writing one's name is a bit young for second- and third-graders, the writing is lovely and the suspense is hard to match!

USE IT TO MODEL: Suspense

The Emperor's New Clothes
by Hans Christian Andersen

SUMMARY: When told by mischievous weavers that his new clothes can only be seen by those with good taste, His Majesty is too vain to admit he can't see the garments.

USE IT TO MODEL: Plot development, character development

If You Give a Mouse a Cookie
by Laura Joffe Numeroff

SUMMARY: A boy learns cause and effect the exhausting way when he realizes what will happen if he gives a bossy mouse a cookie. The book has a fun circular pattern for students to imitate.

USE IT TO MODEL: Circular plot development, organization

Owl Moon
by Jane Yolen

SUMMARY: On a brisk, snowy night, a girl and her dad set out to glimpse and communicate with an owl in the woods.

USE IT TO MODEL: Great beginnings, setting, word choice

Tar Beach
by Faith Ringgold

SUMMARY: While resting on her apartment-building rooftop, an African-American girl dreams of flying over the city.

USE IT TO MODEL: Setting, use of imagery, symbolism

The True Story of the Three Little Pigs
by John Sciezka

SUMMARY: The classic story is retold—this time from the wolf's point of view.

USE IT TO MODEL: Plot development, character development

NONFICTION

Germs Make Me Sick!
by Melvin Berger

SUMMARY: Berger explains how bacteria and viruses spread in common situations and how the body fights back. This book is part of HarperTrophy's Let's-Read-and-Find-Out Science series. Look for other titles in the series as well.

USE IT TO MODEL: Use of detail

Living With Dinosaurs
by Patricia Lauber

SUMMARY: In this trip to Cretaceous-period Montana, readers will glimpse dinosaurs and their neighbors. Reading level may be a bit high for some second-graders.

USE IT TO MODEL: Vibrant language and imagery

The Magic School Bus series
by Joanna Cole and Bruce Degen

SUMMARY: Ms. Frizzle and her class go on all kinds of science adventures aboard their magic bus. Travel with them inside a human body, a beehive, a hurricane, and much more.

USE IT TO MODEL: Use of humor, use of graphs, maps, and other graphic aids

Manners
by Aliki

SUMMARY: A funny examination of how and why to be polite, told in comic-strip fashion.

USE IT TO MODEL: Creative presentation, dialogue

Nature's Green Umbrella: Tropical Rain Forests
by Gail Gibbons

SUMMARY: Gibbons takes a look at the layers of the rain forest and the forest's importance to the global environment.

USE IT TO MODEL: Organization

Sarah Morton's Day
by Kate Waters

SUMMARY: Text and photos taken at Plimoth Plantation follow a Pilgrim girl through a typical day.

USE IT TO MODEL: Organization, use of detail

Does This Book Model Traits of Effective Writing?

Check all that apply.

General

_____ The literature reflects my students' interests.

_____ The literature is at my students' reading level.

_____ The literature demonstrates effective writing traits.

_____ The literature shows respect for men and women and for people of all races, cultures, and ethnicities.

_____ To the best of my knowledge, the details contained in the book are accurate.

Fiction

_____ The story has an interesting plot.

_____ The story is organized with a clear beginning, middle, and ending.

_____ The story demonstrates vivid word choice and imagery.

_____ The story has well-developed characters.

_____ The story has a sense of place and time (setting).

_____ Transition words (suddenly, but, and so on) give the story coherence.

_____ The story has a beginning that hooks the reader.

_____ If the story uses dialogue, it is natural-sounding and lively.

Nonfiction

_____ The book has a clear and focused central topic.

_____ The book is organized around main ideas with supporting details.

_____ The book is well-organized, with sentences, paragraphs, and chapters appearing in an order that makes sense.

_____ The book uses vivid word choice and imagery.

_____ Transition words (*suddenly*, *but*, and so on) give the story coherence.

_____ The book has a beginning that hooks the reader.

_____ The book is reader-friendly, with tools such as photo captions, maps, a table of contents, index, and glossary.

_____ The book is accurate and up-to-date.

Building Skills in Writing: Responding to Literature

Scholastic Professional Books

Do's and Don't's of Good Writing

This bookmark will help you remember various ways to make your writing great. Cut along the dotted lines. Fold in half along the solid line, and glue the bookmark together.

Writing About Books

DON'T:

◎ try to write about a book you did not read.

◎ be embarrassed to say you did not like the book.

◎ start every sentence the same way.

◎ forget to fix spelling and punctuation mistakes.

◎ forget to back up your opinion with details from the book.

Writing About Books

DO:

◎ choose a book at your reading level.

◎ take notes while you're reading.

◎ plan what you want to say about the book.

◎ write in paragraphs.

◎ have a main idea for each paragraph.

The ABC's of Response Journals

You and your students have selected books and started reading. Believe it or not, now is the perfect time to start writing, too! Well before students finish a piece of literature, they can start responding in writing. Even with a relatively brief picture book, there is value in pausing to ask, "What do I think will happen next?" or "Am I enjoying this book as much as I thought I would?" or "What does this book remind me of in my own life?"

An ideal way to get students writing as they read is to have your class keep ongoing literature-response journals. Response journals are flexible tools that you can fine-tune to meet your own unique needs. They are notebooks or diaries in which students record their thoughts and feelings about a piece of literature. Such journals are a way for children to construct personal meaning from literature. The beauty of journaling is that it affords each child the chance to privately explore his or her unique relationship with the book. As John Steinbeck wrote in *The Winter of Our Discontent*:

> A story has as many versions as it has readers, everyone takes what he wants or can from it and thus changes it to his own measure. Some pick out parts and reject the rest, some strain the story through their mesh of prejudice, some paint it with their own delight. A story must have some points of contact with the reader to make him feel at home in it. Only then can he accept its wonders.

Response journals are the perfect place for students to find those "points of contact" with literature that Steinbeck describes. Journals also give students an opportunity to organize their thoughts, integrate new ideas, prepare for class discussions, ask questions, forward opinions, and demonstrate comprehension. The very act of putting response to paper gives concrete shape to ideas and helps students incorporate those ideas into their existing mental framework.

Perhaps the most popular form of literature-response journal is the dialogue journal. In this type of journal, you and the student maintain and record an ongoing dialogue about whatever piece of literature the student is currently reading. The student records his or her thoughts and feelings about the book, then hands the journal in to you. You read the student's entry and offer written comments of your own. These comments should inspire students to think more deeply about the text and to consider ideas and perspectives that might not have occurred to them. You then hand the journal back to the student for another round of "dialogue." Students can address any questions you raised and then start a new response to the book.

Introducing Dialogue Journals to Your Classroom (Use with Kids' Pages 22 and 23.)

1 First, ask each student to bring in a notebook or binder to serve as his or her journal. If using notebooks, I recommend the old-fashioned marble-cover style because these seem to stand up well to repeated openings. If using binders, you can fill the binders with regular looseleaf paper or make copies of the Dialogue Journal template on page 22. You'll need to make one to two copies per student for each writing session. Try making a large batch of copies at once and storing them in an easily accessible spot.

2 Decide how often students will write in their response journals. One idea is to have students write after each free-reading period or each read-aloud. If you prefer and if time permits, designate two days each week as journal days and make time on those days for students to write. These should be days when students are engaged in reading; students should respond to literature as soon as possible to ensure that ideas will be fresh. Allow as much time as you'd like for responding; I suggest starting with ten minutes, then adjusting to suit your needs.

3 Create an atmosphere conducive to reflective writing. Strive for a peaceful, relaxed classroom at journal time. If you have room in your classroom, bring in a few beanbag chairs, pillows, or a plush area rug on which kids can sprawl. Play soft music, and close classroom doors to outside noise.

4 Decide how often you will read and respond to students' journals. You will need to read each student's journal pretty regularly to help keep him or her motivated to write. If you have an especially small class, it is wonderful to review everyone's journal each week. But if you have a large class and little time (as most teachers do), consider creating a journal rotation. Collect five or six journals twice a week, making sure to cover everyone over a two-week period.

5 Provide one or more examples of journal entries for students to read. On page 23, you'll find two sample entries to distribute to students. You might also share a journal entry that you wrote (students often love to see pieces written by their teacher). Emphasize, however, that responses can take many forms. Students should feel free to write whatever they'd like about the text. For

Materials

- multiple copies of Kids' Pages 22 and 23

Protecting Privacy

Before using response journals, explain to students that the contents will not be "published" or shared the way other written projects might be. Journal writings will remain between student and teacher. Occasionally, you may come across a response so insightful that you want to share it with the rest of the class. Be sure to get permission from the writer before doing so. It is also possible that a student may write about a personal experience (such as physical abuse) that gives you cause for concern. Obviously, privacy is a secondary issue in such cases. School and state guidelines should dictate how you follow up.

example, they can tell what they think will happen next or what surprised them about the book they just finished. They can forward opinions about the story or illustrations or even compare the book to others they have read.

6 Encourage children to focus on meaning rather than spelling, mechanics, and grammar. Journal writing is a lot like writing a rough draft of a story or report. Students will eventually create more polished examples of literature response, but at journal time, they should feel free to write earnestly and without the constraints of copyediting.

7 Think carefully about *how* you will respond to students' journal writings. Your responses should show that you care about what each student has to say and that you, too, are thinking about the book. Your responses can also be catalysts to help students delve more deeply into the book. For example, when a student simply retells the story, you can gently encourage him to share opinions or find connections to his own life. For other specific suggestions on responding to children's writings, see What to Expect, below.

What to Expect From Student Entries— and How to Respond (Use with the Teacher Rubric on page 26.)

You will discover that students' response styles will vary tremendously according to personality, writing fluency, interest in the literature, and experience. However, there are several categories of responses that you can expect to see. These include:

1 Retelling or summarizing the story. Many students will use their journal entries to retell the plot, main idea, and/or supporting details from a story. Although retelling demonstrates comprehension, encourage students to go even further in their response journals. In some instances, students summarize parts of the story in order to make other points—for example, to share opinions about the story or to raise new questions. However, you may occasionally find that a student has done nothing more than summarize; he or she has not included any personal reflection. Such an entry may signal that the student does not fully understand the purpose of the response journal or does not enjoy the book. Review the directions with the student, and use dialogue to spur the student to deeper reflection.

For example, if a student writes:

> "In this book, Little Bill goes to the park to sail the little wooden boat he made. The wind makes the boat tip over. It is ruined. Little Bill's friend Kiku tries to give him a paper boat her grandma made, but he doesn't want it. Little Bill doesn't want Kiku to see him cry so he runs home by himself." (Based on *Shipwreck Saturday*, by Bill Cosby.)

You might respond:

"How do you think Little Bill felt when the boat got destroyed? Have you ever felt that way?"

Or, after the student has shown a pattern of simply retelling, you might say, "I am reading along with you, so don't worry about telling me everything that happened. I liked the part when Kiku's grandma made the paper boats. I'd love to learn how to fold paper like that! What was your favorite part?"

2 Raising questions. Questions may be about the plot, vocabulary, characters, illustrations, or other aspects of the book. They are often, but not always, questions that were not answered directly in the story. Such responses demonstrate curiosity and at least some degree of personal meaning-making. In some cases, you may need to directly answer the question. When possible, however, encourage the student to make inferences or to use available resources to answer the question on his or her own.

For example, if a student writes:

"I am confused because it's dark when Chester Raccoon is going to school and it's light when he is home. Does he go to school at night?" (Based on *The Kissing Hand*, by Audrey Penn.)

You might respond:

"Good question! Raccoons are nocturnal. That means they rest during the day and are awake at night. Can you think of any other animals that are like that? (Hint: Look at the next-to-last page for a clue!)"

3 Making inferences about the story. In this type of response, students "read between the lines" of the story to make meaning. Watch for phrases like "must be" or "is probably." These are clues that a student is going beyond material that is stated explicitly in the text and is using his or her higher-order thinking skills. With some pieces of literature, students may even infer a lesson or moral. Be aware that students sometimes infer ideas that are clearly not supported by the text. In such cases, invite the student to look back to the text for substantiation.

For example, if a student writes:

"Poor Alexander! He is having a bad day and then his mom makes him go to the dentist. Yuck! She must be mad at him." (Based on *Alexander and the Terrible, Horrible, No Good, Very Bad Day*, by Judith Viorst.)

You might respond:

"There's a picture of Alexander and his mom at the dentist's office in the book. Do you think she looks mad? Might there be another reason she took Alexander and his brothers to the dentist?"

4 **Making predictions about the story.** When writing a journal entry in the middle of reading a chapter book or longer picture book, students may try to guess what will happen next. This is particularly fun to do with suspense stories and stories with surprise endings. Making predictions is a wonderful indication that the student is fully engaged in the story and eager to keep reading. When responding to students, don't hesitate to make your own predictions (or to tell what you thought would happen the *first* time you read the book, since you've probably read it over and over by now and you don't want to give away the plotline). You might also encourage the student to support his or her prediction with evidence from the text or with sound logic.

For example, if a student writes:

> "Arthur has a hard job to do. He has to get someone to be the turkey in the play. I bet Francine does it because they are best friends." (Based on *Arthur's Thanksgiving*, by Marc Brown.)

You might respond:

> "Hmmm…interesting prediction. What has Francine said about it so far? Would you be willing to play a turkey if your best friend asked you to? I think I would do it!"

5 **Sharing opinions.** Students may have strong feelings about the story, characters, illustrations, or writing style. These opinions can be positive, negative, or even mixed. Look to see whether the student has supported his or her opinion with examples or evidence from the text. If so, commend the student for using this writing strategy. If not, suggest that the student refer to the text or to personal experience to support his or her view.

For example, if a student writes:

> "Half of me does want animals to be free because they are supposed to be in the wild. The other half wants them to stay in the circus because there is no circus without animals." (Based on a children's magazine article about circus animals.)

You might respond:

> "I understand how you can feel both ways at the same time. What could circuses do to entertain people without using animals?"

6 **Intertextual connections.** In this type of response, students draw comparisons or connections between the text they have just read and information they have acquired from books, television, newspapers, or other media. You can encourage a thoughtful response by providing a wide variety of books and other resources for children to enjoy.

For example, if a student writes:

"I liked that other Magic School Bus book about the human body but this one is even better. I'd rather go into space than travel inside a body. I noticed that this time, Ms. Frizzle wore a dress with space stuff on it." (Based on *The Magic School Bus Lost in the Solar System*, by Joanna Cole and Bruce Degen.)

You might respond:

"It sounds like you really get excited about space! I found a magazine article about comets you might like to read at our next Drop Everything and Read time. I'll bring it in for you."

7 **Personal connections.** Students can often relate stories to their own experiences, interests, and backgrounds. There are actually several distinct styles of response within this category, including statements of emotion (anger, sadness, and so on), statements relating the text to one's own interests or experiences, and statements putting oneself in the context of the story (for example, "If I were that character, I would…"). I feel that this is one of the most important types of literature response, for it shows that a student has truly interacted with the book.

For example, if a student writes:

"This story reminds me of my cousin Cecilia. She used to live down the street from me, but she moved last year. I was a little mad and a lot sad when she left. Amber probably feels that way about Justin leaving." (Based on *Amber Brown Is Not a Crayon*, by Paula Danziger.)

You might respond:

"It must be hard to have a friend move away. What advice would you give Amber if you could talk to her?"

Make copies of the Teacher Rubric on page 26. This rubric provides an easy way to keep notes on how well each of your students is responding to literature.

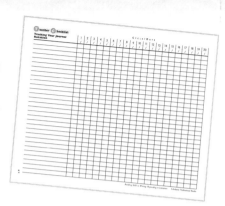

Tracking Your Journal Rotation

(Use with the Teacher Checklist on page 27.)

This grid will help you keep track of whose journals you have read. A journal cycle can be whatever time period you designate. It is the length of time it takes to dialogue with every student in the class—typically about two weeks. Put a check next to each student's name once you've read his or her journal in that cycle.

Side Trips: Other Types of Journaling

Want to try something new? Use these types of journals as substitutes for the traditional dialogue journal.

Buddy Journal *(Use with Kids' Page 22.)*

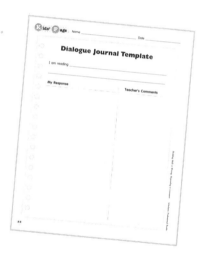

Buddy journals are dialogue journals in which students converse with one another, rather than with the teacher. You can use the template on page 22, but invite students to exchange journals with a designated partner who is reading the same piece of literature. Emphasize that all writing must pertain to the book, and that students must respect each other's thoughts and feelings in each entry. You'll want to collect buddy journals periodically to make sure each student is following the directions and getting the feedback he or she needs.

Materials

● copy of Kids' Page 22 for each student

Predict-and-Check Journal

(Use with Kids' Page 24.)

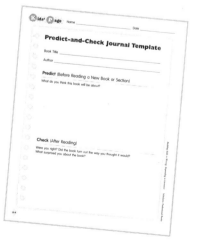

In this type of journal, the student pauses before reading a new picture book or a chapter in a chapter book and writes what he or she thinks will happen. Then, at the next writing session, he or she notes whether the predictions were on track and makes new predictions for the chapter or pages to come. It's your role to provide feedback about each student's predictions; you will probably write fewer and less elaborate comments than you would in a dialogue journal.

Materials

● copy of Kids' Page 24 for each student

"Virtual Reality" Journal

Since I was a child, I have loved getting so immersed in a story that I actually start to think like the central character. I temporarily suspend my own reality and, as long as outside distractions are minimal, I live in the story. You can encourage students to get similarly swept away by having them keep journals from the perspective of a favorite character in the story they are currently reading. You might try this for a single journal session or for a whole week. It works best when students are comfortable with journal-keeping in general. With this type of journal, students imagine that they are the character writing in a diary. To write successfully, they must ask: "What would this character think about the way the plot is developing? What would he or she think about the other characters? How might he or she phrase her thoughts?" Such journal entries are a fantastic way to develop writing skills such as character development, voice, and dialogue. These journals are especially fun to use when reading works of historical fiction.

Prompt-a-Day Idea Cube (Use with Kids' Page 25.)

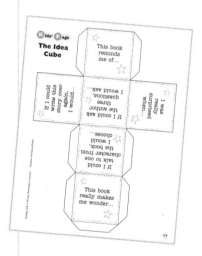

Have students roll an Idea Cube to pick a ready-to-use writing prompt. If students are still warming up to the idea of response journals and are looking for some guidance, consider providing a prompt each day for students to respond to. You can write a single prompt on the chalkboard and ask all students to write to the same prompt, or you can invite each student to choose a prompt independently. Responding to prompts will give students practice in writing about literature; soon they will be coming up with original response ideas of their own. To get started, try using the Idea Cube—a make-it-yourself paper die with a different writing prompt on each side. Students will have as much fun making it as they will using it! Here's how to construct the cube:

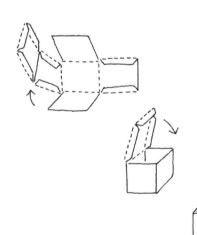

◎ Direct students to cut out the pattern along the outer solid lines.

◎ Have them fold in along the dotted lines to form a cube.

◎ Next, show students how to tape down the flaps.

◎ Finally, have students roll the cube and use the prompt on top to start writing in their journals.

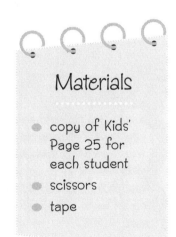

Materials

● copy of Kids' Page 25 for each student

● scissors

● tape

Dialogue Journal Template

I am reading _____

_____

My Response	Teacher's Comments

Building Skills in Writing: Responding to Literature   Scholastic Professional Books

Sample Journal Entries

Entry 1

Name __Alexandra Vogel__   Date __February 24__

Dialogue Journal Template

I am reading __The Principal's New Clothes,__
__by Stephanie Calmenson__

My Response

I just have a few pages to go
in this book. It is really a lot of
laughs!

This book is like the book The
Emperor's New Clothes which
we read at the beginning of the
year. In that story, people are
trying to fool the emperor,
and in this one people are
trying to fool the principal. One
happens in a palace, and the
other one happens in a school.
Except for those things, they
are the same.

I think it's funny that the
principal won't admit that he
can't see his new suit. He must
be pretty stuck on himself. I
wonder if he'll find out the
truth about his suit!

Teacher's Comments

Entry 2

Name __Liam Savona__   Date __October 18__

Dialogue Journal Template

I am reading __Tar Beach, by Faith Ringgold__

My Response

I read this whole book today
during free reading time. At
first I thought it was going to
be about a real beach, but then
I noticed the pictures were not
of sand and stuff like that. I
really liked the book but I am
still not sure why it's called
Tar Beach.

My favorite part is when
Cassie dreams of flying over
the big bridge her father helped
build. I liked that part because
I felt like I was flying with
Cassie. I also liked that part
because you can tell she is
really proud of her dad.

If I could fly anywhere, I would
fly over the stadium during a
baseball game and watch the
game for free!

Teacher's Comments

Predict-and-Check Journal Template

Book Title _____

Author _____

Predict (Before Reading a New Book or Section)

What do you think this book will be about?

Check (After Reading)

Were you right? Did the book turn out the way you thought it would?
What surprised you about the book?

Building Skills in Writing: Responding to Literature   Scholastic Professional Books

The Idea Cube

This book reminds me of...

If I could write this story over again, I would...

If I could ask the author three questions, I would ask...

I was really surprised when...

If I could talk to one character from the book, I would choose...

This book really makes me wonder...

How Well Are My Students Responding to Literature?

Student's Name

_____

Date _____

How often does the student...

Summarize information from the book?	frequently	sometimes	never
Raise questions about plot, characters, or other aspects of the book?	frequently	sometimes	never
Make inferences from the text or illustrations?	frequently	sometimes	never
Make predictions about the book?	frequently	sometimes	never
Express opinions about the book?	frequently	sometimes	never
Support opinions with evidence from the book?	frequently	sometimes	never
Make connections between the book and other books and media?	frequently	sometimes	never
Make connections between the book and his or her own life?	frequently	sometimes	never

My Notes on _____'s Progress in Responding to Literature:

_____

_____

_____

_____

_____

_____

_____

Tracking Your Journal Rotation

Cycle/Date

1/	2/	3/	4/	5/	6/	7/	8/	9/	10/	11/	12/	13/	14/	15/	16/	17/	18/	19/	20/

3

Other Creative Ways to Respond to Literature

As discussed in chapter 2, response journals are a wonderful way to keep kids writing about what they read all year long. But it's also important to provide other types of literature-response opportunities. Unlike entries in a journal, which are relatively private and informal, the activities in this chapter require students to work through the stages of the writing process, from prewriting to proofreading. The finished products are meant to be published or shared with others in the classroom or larger community.

The lessons that follow will help you teach about plot and character development, organization, setting, dialogue, and other components of good literature. Understanding and appreciating these elements through literature response is an important step toward writing original stories and reports of one's own.

It's a Cover-Up!
(Creating Book Jackets)

WRITING SKILLS Students will summarize, identify a pivotal scene or main idea, advance judgments about the text, and understand the importance of presentation.

How do you select a book to read? You probably check out the jacket information. Book jackets can tell us a great deal about what's inside. A jacket illustration often highlights a key scene or character, and a short summary reveals the basic plotline. Publishers may also put quotes from reviewers or excerpts from the story itself on the jacket to catch readers' attention.

Integrate the enjoyment of reading good literature with a real-life writing activity by inviting students to make new jackets for worn and dusty titles in your school or classroom library. Many books have probably lost their jackets over time; others, like paperbacks and library bindings, may never have had jackets to start with. These books could use a little tender loving care to make them attractive to readers once again. In the process, your students will learn some strategies for effective writing.

Materials

- large sheets of high-quality construction paper or craft paper
- scissors
- markers and crayons
- scrap paper
- computer (with word-processing software so that students can type their work and paste it onto the jacket, if desired)

Prewriting

◎ Read the worn books and have each student choose one.

◎ Ask students to take notes about important characters and scenes.

Writing and Revising

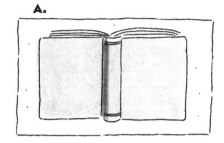

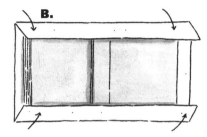

1 Measure each book jacket to fit. Fold the top and bottom edges of the paper in as shown, then fold the jacket over the front and back covers of the book. Trim the left and right edges of the jacket if it is too long for the book. Finally, slide the front and back book covers into the sleeves created by the folded paper. Voila!

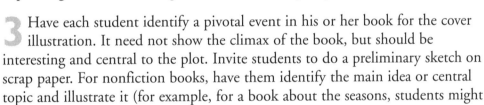

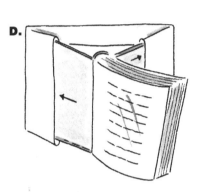

2 Direct students to write the book title, author, and illustrator in large type in a prominent spot on the front jacket. (They might plan this out on scrap paper first.) Encourage children to try different typefaces depending on the mood or genre of the book (mystery, adventure, and so on).

3 Have each student identify a pivotal event in his or her book for the cover illustration. It need not show the climax of the book, but should be interesting and central to the plot. Invite students to do a preliminary sketch on scrap paper. For nonfiction books, have them identify the main idea or central topic and illustrate it (for example, for a book about the seasons, students might draw four panels showing the changing weather).

4 For the back of the jacket, each student should write a brief but captivating summary of his or her book's plot on scrap paper. Remind students to provide just enough detail to attract readers' interest. And, of course, don't give away any surprise endings! Each summary should be about four to six sentences.

5 Beneath the summary, students should each include a quote from a book reviewer (themselves, of course!). Because students have chosen books they like, quotes will obviously be positive. But encourage students to be specific. For example, for a biography of Michael Jordan, "Sports fans will love the photos in this action-packed book!" works better than "This book is very good."

Editing and Publishing

Help students edit and proofread their work, then create final versions. If you'd like, use clear contact paper to protect the book jackets. Encourage children to read the jackets when deciding which book to read next.

Character Cards

WRITING SKILLS Students will explore character development.

As toy marketers know, 7- to 9-year-olds love just about anything they can collect and trade—from baseball cards to Pokemon® paraphernalia. Why not tap into this enthusiasm for your reading and writing curriculum? In this activity, students will create trading cards for characters from the literature they read. In doing so, they will learn how an author paints a picture of a character through descriptions, dialogue, action, and other story elements. This knowledge will help students create more vivid characters in their own writing.

Prewriting

◎ Decide which book you will use for this activity. It should be one with several main characters.

◎ Have children discuss the characters in small groups. Invite each student to pick one character to start.

Writing and Revising

1 Make multiple copies of the Character Cards reproducible on page 31. Cut the cards apart and give one to each student. Invite each student to draw the character he or she has chosen on the blank side of the card.

2 Have students fill in their cards with pertinent information about the characters that they have chosen. The "stats" for each character include name, age, appearance, likes and dislikes, and a quote from the book. Keep in mind that some books—even some with excellent character development—do not provide all of these details about their characters. When that happens, have students use their imagination to make inferences to answer the questions. For example, a picture book may not tell you exactly how old a character is. Have children consider the character's behavior and consult illustrations before making an educated guess.

3 Give students additional Character Cards for them to fill in for other book characters.

Editing and Publishing

Have students edit and proofread their cards and then create more polished finished versions. You may wish to mat the cards on cardboard so they'll stand up to handling. (In that case, paste the picture on one side and the character information on the other.)

Materials

- copies of Kids' Page 31
- scissors
- markers or crayons
- cardboard (optional)
- glue sticks (optional)

Extending Learning

Make a mobile with all the character cards for one book. Punch a hole in the top of each card and use string to hang the cards (at varying lengths) from a wire clothes hanger.

Character Cards

Name: _____

Age: _____

Appearance: _____

Likes: _____

Dislikes: _____

Quote from book: _____

Other interesting information: _____

Name: _____

Age: _____

Appearance: _____

Likes: _____

Dislikes: _____

Quote from book: _____

Other interesting information: _____

Book Talk—
A Literature Talk Show

WRITING SKILLS Students will explore plot and character development and practice writing dialogue.

What would Harry Potter say if he were interviewed on television? What probing questions might an investigative reporter ask Lyle the Crocodile? Here's your students' chance to decide! In this activity, students will take turns role-playing talk show hosts and characters from favorite books. As hosts, they'll generate lists of thought-provoking questions to ask their "bookish" guests. Then students will trade papers and answer classmates' questions from the characters' point of view.

Prewriting

- Have students work with a partner (both students must have read the same book).

- Discuss the format of a talk show or interview.

- Explain that interviewers usually prepare questions in advance based on what they want to find out. Provide examples of effective, open-ended questions and boring yes-or-no questions. Discuss.

Writing and Revising

1 After completing the book, have students form pairs. Invite each student to first take a turn as interviewer or talk show host. That student then chooses a character from the book to invite on the "show."

2 Distribute the Book Talk reproducible, and have each student list his or her questions for the character.

3 Roam the room and help each student fine-tune his or her questions. Eliminate conversation-stumpers (such as "What is your name?" or "Do you like being an aardvark?") in favor of open-ended questions (such as "What kinds of things make you mad?" or "How did you enjoy your recent adventure?").

4 Direct students to trade papers. Have each student pretend to be his or her partner's guest. Students should write answers to the questions as they think the character would respond, not as they themselves would.

Publishing

Create a "set" in the front of your classroom (two chairs will do just fine!) and pretend to tape an episode of the talk show. Invite each pair of students to read aloud their questions and answers for the whole class.

Materials

- copy of Kids' Page 33 for each pair of students

Book Talk—
A Literature Talk Show

My name _____ My partner's name _____

Today I am interviewing the character _____ ,

from the book _____ .

1 My question: _____
_____

Character's answer: _____
_____
_____

2 My question: _____
_____

Character's answer: _____
_____
_____

3 My question: _____
_____

Character's answer: _____
_____
_____

4 My question: _____
_____

Character's answer: _____
_____
_____

Materials

- book in which the plot builds toward a central conflict or event. Examples: *Goldilocks and the Three Bears* or *Cinderella*, or a modern story like Vera Williams's *A Chair for My Mother* (in which a little girl saves to buy her mom a special chair), or Ezra Jack Keats's *Apt. 3* (in which two brothers set out to uncover who is playing the harmonica in their apartment building).

Don't Let It End This Way!

WRITING SKILLS Students will explore plot, particularly the use of effective endings.

One way to help students feel like successful writers is to let them ride the coattails of an author they admire. In this lesson I suggest two simple ways to do just that: by writing new endings and sequels for stories they've enjoyed. These strategies will give students practice in developing plots—and a chance to see how real authors do it.

New Endings

Prewriting

- Read the book you have chosen several times.
- Discuss what makes the story funny, interesting, moving, or otherwise engaging.

Writing and Revising

1 Read the book again. This time, have students stop at a predetermined page. This spot can be anywhere in the book, as long as it is before the story reveals its conclusion. For example, in the story of Goldilocks, you might stop reading when Goldilocks falls asleep. Say, "We all know how the story really ends, but now let's have some fun writing new endings. If it were up to you, how would you finish the story?"

2 Invite students to draft their endings, emphasizing that endings are not whole new stories (students may try to steer the tale in a whole new direction; save this for writing sequels, page 35).

Editing and Publishing

Point out that even published authors rarely write a knock-your-socks-off ending in one shot. Encourage students to rewrite until they are pleased with the final product. After students have edited and proofread their work, read the story aloud once more, again stopping at the preselected spot. Encourage willing students to read aloud their endings. Compare the styles of different endings.

Sequels

Prewriting

◎ Read aloud an example of a book with its "sequel," such as the classic fairy tale *The Three Little Pigs* and *The True Story of the Three Little Pigs*, by John Scieszka. Explain that for our purposes, a sequel is a story that revolves around the same character(s) as the original. It may take up where the original left off, tell the original story through a new set of eyes, or present the characters in a whole new situation.

◎ Discuss movies with sequels.

◎ Have students select books for which they would like to write sequels.

Writing and Revising

1 As students get to work, roam the room or arrange a brief story conference with each student. Find out what approach each student is taking for his or her sequel.

2 Remind students to give their sequels interesting titles. (If students choose to use numbers, such as *Cinderella II*, encourage them to also include a subtitle. EXAMPLE: *Cinderella II: Stepmother Visits the Castle*.) Many students will find it easier to write the title first, then start the story, since this forces them to focus on a central idea.

Editing and Publishing

Using the student checklist on page 54, have students edit their own and each other's work. When stories are in final form, encourage students to make construction paper covers and staple the edges together. Display the sequels with the originals in your classroom library, and invite students to read their classmates' work just as they would any other book.

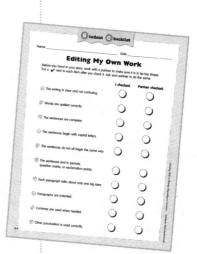

Materials

- book in which the plot follows a predictable, cumulative, or circular pattern. Examples: *If You Give a Mouse a Cookie* (or its sequels, all by Laura Joffe Numeroff) or *We're Going on a Bear Hunt* (Michael Rosen)

Extending Learning

Invite students to write their own "plot-pattern puzzle" stories using a particular plot pattern. Then let students share their story with the class. Can classmates identify the plot pattern used in each story?

Plot-Pattern Puzzle

WRITING SKILLS Students will explore plot patterns.

When my oldest daughter was three, I noticed that she could "read" her favorite picture book—*If You Give a Mouse a Cookie*—almost verbatim. The book has a predictable, circular plot that made it easy for her to memorize the text. Later I realized those same plot qualities would make it easy for emergent writers to copy the style of the book. In this activity your students will do just that—imitate the plots of certain predictable picture books. Just as my daughter felt successful as a reader, your students will feel successful as writers.

Prewriting

◎ Read aloud the book you have chosen several times.

◎ Ask, "What do you notice about this story?" Explain that you are going to imitate that pattern in your own class story.

Writing and Revising

1 As a class, decide how you are going to approach the plot pattern. Begin by adapting the story title according to student suggestions. For example, you might change *If You Give a Mouse a Cookie* to *If You Give a Bear a Berry*. You could change *We're Going on a Bear Hunt* to *We're Going on an Apple-Picking Trip*. Have kids use their imagination.

2 When they've settled on a title, draft the story together on chart paper or on the chalkboard. Use the basic plot structure of the book you're using as a model, including any repetitive clauses. For example, in the story *If You Give a Mouse a Cookie*, the author uses an amusing "If… then…" pattern throughout the story, eventually bringing the tale back to the situation that got the whole thing started ("If you give a mouse a cookie, he's going to want some milk to go with it. If you give him some milk…" and so on).

Editing and Publishing

When you're through, read the new story aloud. Invite students to make any desired changes in the content and to hunt for spelling mistakes and other errors. Rewrite the story, spreading it out over several pages so that children can illustrate it.

Scene-Setting Travel Brochure

WRITING SKILLS Students will explore setting.

Imagine visiting some of the wonderful settings described in literature. You could experience 1920s Harlem as it is described in Faith Ringgold's *Tar Beach*, go on a country owl-watching expedition like the one in Jane Yolen's *Owl Moon*, or even stop to take pictures of *The Biggest Sandwich Ever* at a roadside park (I'm sure author Rita Gelman would be thrilled to see her sandwich became a tourist attraction!). In this activity, students will use their imagination to create travel brochures for favorite story settings. In the process, they'll learn how important setting can be to a story and uncover some professional authors' tricks for establishing this sense of place and time.

Prewriting

◎ Bring in some travel brochures from an agency to share with students. Discuss the types of information they contain (descriptions of weather or climate, sites to see, things to do, interesting facts about the place).

◎ Have students select books to use. Encourage them to read the book twice. The second time through, encourage students to put sticky notes on pages with descriptions or illustrations of the story's setting.

◎ Explain that setting is not just a place but also a time. Some books have the reader travel in time. Students can have fun incorporating the element of time travel (past or future) into their brochures.

Writing and Revising

Distribute a double-sided copy of the Scene-Setting Travel Brochure reproducible to each student. First, have students cut out the brochure along the outer dotted lines. Then demonstrate how to fold the paper accordion-style. (This is called a trifold.)

Materials

● books with strong descriptions of setting
● double-sided copy of Kids' Pages 39 and 40 for each student
● scissors
● markers and crayons

Extending Learning

Although the examples cited above are all fiction, this lesson works equally well with nonfiction literature about communities, states, countries, ecosystems, and other interesting places. For example, students might create a travel brochure about Canada, the rain forest, or Yellowstone National Park.

2 Have students fill in all the sections of the brochure with descriptions of their book's setting. They'll use evidence from the book and their imagination to describe what a visitor to that place might see, hear, taste, smell, and do. They'll also practice using adjectives to describe the setting.

3 Invite students to draw colorful illustrations to go with each description.

Editing and Publishing

Remind students to check to make sure they spelled and capitalized words correctly and used appropriate punctuation. Then make the brochures the focus of an exciting bulletin board or display table titled "Literature Takes You Places."

Visit

Draw a picture of the setting.

the place made famous in the book

_____ (book title)

by _____ (author)

1

Draw a picture.

6

Don't miss out. Visit now! This place sure is

(On the lines below, list five adjectives that describe the setting.)

Draw a picture of people enjoying the setting.

There is plenty to do here.

You can _____

and _____

5

You might see _____
_____
_____
_____
or some _____
_____
_____ .

Draw some things you might see in this setting.

2

You might hear _____
_____
_____
or _____
_____
_____
_____ .

Draw some things you might hear in this setting.

3

You might even taste a. _____
_____
_____
or smell the _____
_____
_____ .

Draw some things you might taste or smell in this setting.

4

Building Skills in Writing: Responding to Literature   Scholastic Professional Books

What's the Word?
(Creating Text for Wordless Books)

WRITING SKILLS Students will explore plot and character development and practice writing dialogue.

Materials

- wordless picture book. Examples: Raymond Briggs's *The Snowman* or Eric Carle's *Do You Want to Be My Friend?*

Do your students need a jump start on the writing process? Try using a wordless picture book to spark creative writing. Invite students to create text and dialogue to go with the existing illustrations.

Prewriting

◎ Have students study and enjoy the illustrations and take notes on what is happening in the story. Invite them to assign names to the characters pictured in the book.

Writing and Revising

1 As a first draft, have students simply write the story down frame by frame. (EXAMPLE: "The boy woke up and went to the window. He saw snow on the ground.") Note that students will have different interpretations of the pictures. That's wonderful! It will make each written story unique.

2 Now have students refine their stories, adding descriptive words, dialogue, and names. (EXAMPLE: Tony stretched lazily. Then he headed over to his bedroom window. "Wow!" he said to himself. "Just look at all that snow!")

Editing and Publishing

After students have edited and revised their stories, read aloud several student stories each day for a week. Or arrange for students to read their stories to children in a kindergarten or first-grade class.

Plot Pop-Up Book

WRITING SKILLS Students will identify and explore story beginnings, middles, and endings.

As much as children love a good story, they are frequently not consciously aware of the structural elements of a story—a catchy beginning, suspenseful or action-packed middle, and satisfying ending. Becoming more familiar with these story parts (and the amazing variety of ways authors tackle them) will help students successfully structure their own stories.

Materials

- double-sided copy of Kids' Pages 43 and 44 for each student
- scissors
- markers or crayons

Prewriting

◎ Have students select and read a book to summarize.

◎ Challenge students to find the beginning, middle, and ending of the book. Although the beginning and ending should be easy to locate, the middle may be more elusive. In this case, when we speak of the middle of the story, we mean the central conflict or event—the "meat" of the story.

Writing and Revising

1 Distribute double-sided copies of the Plot Pop-Up Book reproducibles. With side A faceup, direct students to fold the page in half along the solid line.

2 Instruct students to fill in the titles and authors of the books they have read. Then invite them to write descriptions of the beginnings, middles, and endings of the stories. Have students illustrate each segment as well.

3 Finally, have students cut along the horizontal dotted lines to create flaps.

Extending Learning

If students worked with different books, discuss the varied ways authors approached the beginnings, middles, and endings of their stories. Ask, "What were some ways writers started their books?" "Were all of the story middles about problems? How many books had surprise endings?"

Editing and Publishing

Meet briefly with each student to discuss his or her "pop-up plot," paying attention to how well each student understood the structure of the story. Some students will want or need to go back and redo their work. When everyone is happy with the final product, display students' work on a bulletin board titled "Open the Door to a Great Plot."

Plot Pop-Up Book

_____

Book title

_____

Book author

Lift the flaps to describe your book's
beginning, middle, and ending.

A good book
has a **beginning**
that catches
your attention.

→

The **middle** of the book is where the
action or problem happens.

→

At the **ending**
of a book,
the problem
gets solved
or the action
ends.

In the beginning of this book...

_____

_____

_____

_____

In the middle of this book...

_____

_____

_____

_____

At the ending of this book...

_____

_____

_____

_____

Building Skills in Writing: Responding to Literature

Scholastic Professional Books

Dear Author...
(Writing to Favorite Authors)

Materials

- paper, envelopes, stamps (or access to e-mail and author's e-mail address)

WRITING SKILLS Students will advance judgments about literature, support judgments with references to text, and raise questions about literature.

One natural way for students to respond to what they read is to write to the author or illustrator. This helps children see authors as real people and gives a real-life purpose and context to literature response. Even when an author is no longer living (or when no contact information can be found), students benefit from putting their feedback into written form.

Prewriting

◎ Have students select a favorite book and search for information about its author. Students can write to many authors through their publishing companies; find the publisher and address in the front of each book. With your help, students can also find addresses and e-mail addresses by logging on to the Internet. Try, for example, **www.cbcbooks.org** (the Children's Book Council site with links to many authors' home pages) or **www.scils.rutgers.edu/special/kay/author.html** (another site with links to author pages, maintained by a Rutgers University professor).

Writing and Revising

1 You might have students begin this activity individually, with everyone writing to the same author. Have students write their (polite!) opinions about the author's work, backing up opinions with examples or evidence from the book (for example, "I think you are great at describing things. I love the way you describe the still, dark night in *Owl Moon*."). Students can also ask questions about the text that can be answered only by the author (for example, "How did you get the idea for this book?").

2 Although you can send 25 different letters to an author, that's probably not the best way to get on the author's good side! Instead, combine the students' individual letters into one. Invite each student to contribute one opinion or question, and list these (along with the name of each contributor) after a friendly opening paragraph.

Editing and Publishing

Have students form three teams: (1) Organizers; (2) Editors; and (3) Rewriters. The organizers are responsible for compiling the joint letter and putting students' comments and questions in an order that makes sense. The editors then check the letter for spelling, punctuation, and capitalization, marking their suggested changes on the manuscript in red. Finally, the rewriters carefully copy the letter, incorporating the final edits, or, if you used a computer, insert the final edits into the word-processing document. NOTE: If you make author letters a standard part of your literature-response repertoire, be sure to rotate your team assignments.

Story-Spinner Wheel

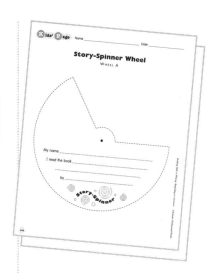

WRITING SKILLS Students will further explore plot, character development, and setting.

In this activity, students synthesize what they've learned about the elements of a story. Students will create rotating wheels to describe the plot, setting, and characters of the book they read.

Prewriting

◎ Have students select and read a fiction book.

Writing and Revising

Distribute copies of the Story-Spinner reproducibles. Using a book you've read aloud to the class, demonstrate how to write about each story element in the three frames of the circle. Each frame has a prompt to guide students:

Plot: Describe what happened in the story.
Characters: Describe two important characters in the story.
Setting: Describe the place where the story happens.

Editing and Publishing

Provide as many copies of the reproducible as students need to make revisions. When students are happy with their work, have them cut out the two pieces that make up the spinner. Direct them to put wheel A on top of wheel B, and secure with a brass fastener. Students can then decorate the front of the spinner with illustrations of favorite scenes or characters from the book. To read and share the spinner, simply turn the top circle to expose each frame.

Materials

- copies of Kids' Pages 48 and 49 for each student
- extra copies for revisions
- scissors
- brass fasteners
- markers and crayons

Name _____ Date _____

Story-Spinner Wheel

WHEEL A

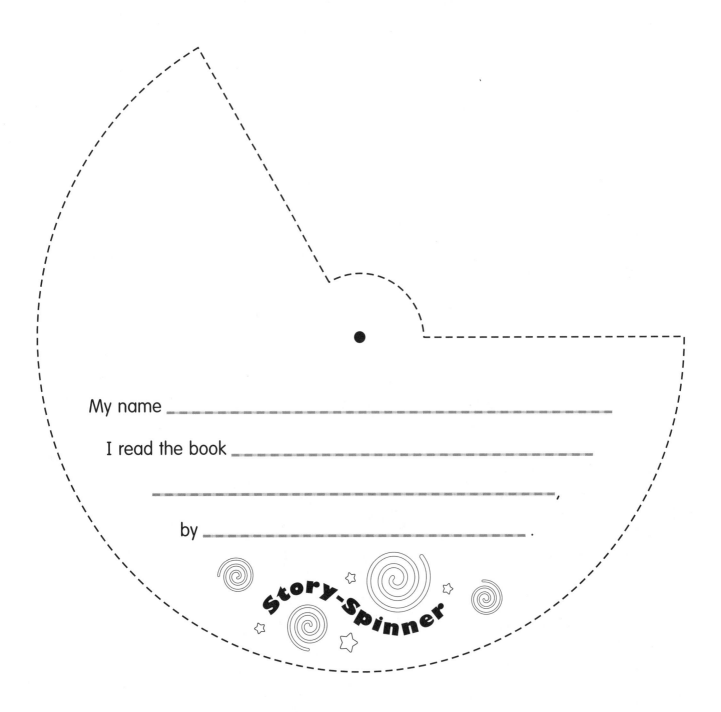

My name _____

I read the book _____

_____,

by _____.

Story-Spinner

Building Skills in Writing: Responding to Literature

Scholastic Professional Books

Story-Spinner Wheel

Wheel B

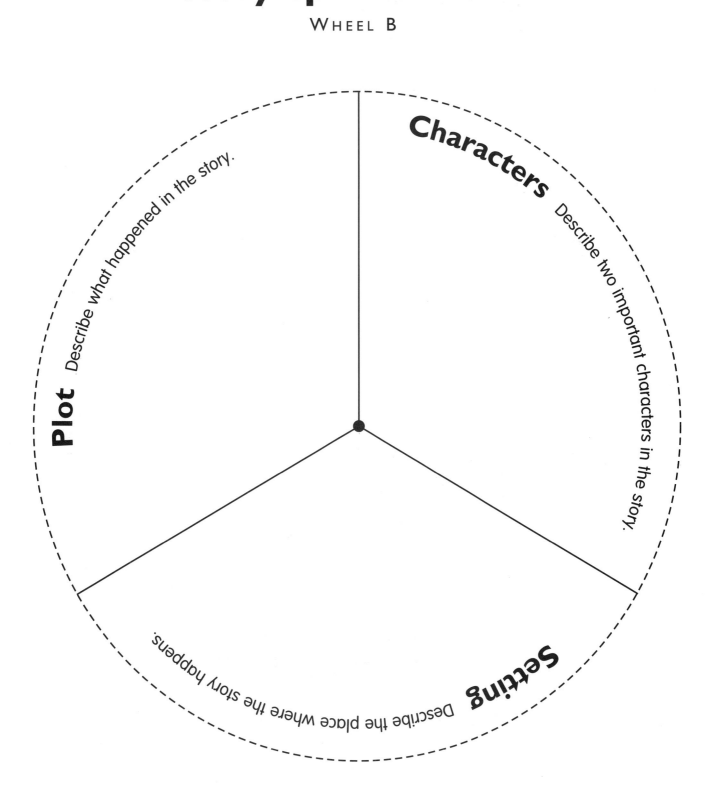

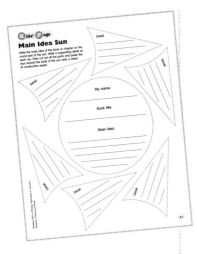

Main Idea Sun

WRITING SKILLS Students will identify main idea and supporting details in nonfiction literature.

Well-written nonfiction always centers on an identifiable main idea. In this activity, students will practice finding and summarizing the main idea in nonfiction books and articles, as well as locating the details and examples that support each main idea. To help students understand and remember the relationship between main ideas and details, they can use a friendly image of the sun.

Materials

- copies of Kids' Page 51 for each student (If possible, use light yellow or orange paper to make the suns colorful.)
- scissors
- glue stick
- contrasting color construction paper

Prewriting

◎ Have students select and read a nonfiction book on any topic.

◎ If the book is a chapter book, have the student select one chapter to focus on. (In most informational chapter books, each chapter has a new main idea.)

Writing and Revising

1 Distribute copies of the Main-Idea Sun reproducible. Using a book you've read as a model, show students how to write the main idea of the book in the main part of the sun. Explain that the main idea is what the book or chapter is all about.

2 Now show students how to write supporting details and examples on the six rays of the sun. Point out that students need not fill in all six details if the book or chapter they've read is very short.

3 Have students glue the sun and rays to construction paper. If a student has not properly identified a main idea or has confused a main idea with a detail, help him or her understand the activity and try again.

Editing and Publishing

Instruct students to make sure that all of their main ideas and details are written as complete sentences with appropriate punctuation and capitalization. Students can check one another's work. Publish the projects on a bulletin board about nonfiction literature. Simply staple the suns around an exciting, related title such as "Nonfiction Books Shed Some Light on Things" or "Main Ideas Help Books Shine."

Kids' Page

Main Idea Sun

Write the main idea of the book or chapter on the round part of the sun. Write a supporting detail on each ray. Then cut out all the parts and paste the rays around the body of the sun onto a sheet of construction paper.

Detail:

_____

_____

_____

Detail:

Detail:

Detail:

Detail:

Detail:

Detail:

My name:

_____

Book title:

_____

Main idea:

_____

_____

_____

_____

_____

Building Skills in Writing: Responding to Literature
Scholastic Professional Books

Wrapping Up Literature-Response Projects: Suggestions for Editing, Publishing, and Assessing

Many specific tips for editing, publishing, and assessing students' response to literature are found in the preceding chapters. The following are some additional general suggestions, checklists, and rubrics to assist you and your students in the final stages of the writing process.

Editing

Once students have drafted and revised their work, allow a day or two of "breathing" time before moving on to the editing stage. That will give students a chance to return to their work with more objective eyes. (When we've read our own work over and over again, we tend to see what we *think* is there rather than what is actually there. By distancing ourselves for a while, we are more likely to see any mistakes or weaknesses.)

I also recommend that students pair up for one or more peer editing sessions. Peer editors can use the Editing My Own Work checklist on page 54 to help pinpoint any errors or omissions in the work. Although peer editors can use traditional editing symbols (see page 55) to edit directly on a writer's paper, they should use pencil just in case the edits are incorrect. Although computer word-processing programs make it easy to print out a story or project over and over again, a student who has hand-written his or her project will not be pleased to have to rewrite it unnecessarily. If a writer and peer editor disagree on an edit, have them come to you for clarification. Student writers should hand in a copy of the editing checklist along with their final projects to show that they completed the self-editing and peer-editing processes.

Publishing

Celebrate literature and writing by dedicating a corner or wall of your classroom to current literature projects. Display the books students have read, along with completed projects relating to those books. For example, you might display Ezra Jack Keats's wordless book *The Snowy Day* near students' own versions of the story. Connecting "real" literature to students' own writing will help them feel like accomplished authors.

Assessment

Of course, literature-response journals serve as year-round authentic assessment tools. These journals are a window into how your students are responding to literature and how much thought and skill they are dedicating to their own writing. You can also assess what students are learning by keeping individual portfolios. Work with each student to select items for his or her writing portfolio, paying special attention to those the student is especially proud of and those that show growth over time. (For example, you might select both the first and final draft of a favorite book review to show how the student used the stages of the writing process to fine-tune his or her piece.) Parents will enjoy browsing through their child's literature-response portfolio at conference time, and you'll have an ongoing testament to each student's progress.

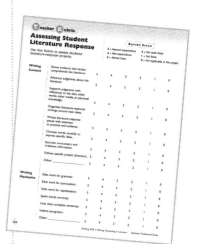

Still another valuable tool for assessing students' responses to literature is a rubric that allows you to rate each facet of a student's work. On page 56, you'll find a rubric designed to help you assess both content and mechanics in nearly any literature response project. You may copy and use the rubric as is or adapt it to suit your individual needs.

Name _____ Date _____

Editing My Own Work

Before you hand in your story, work with a partner to make sure it is in tip-top shape. Put a ✔ next to each item after you check it. Ask your partner to do the same.

	I checked.	Partner checked.
The writing is clear and not confusing.	◯	◯
Words are spelled correctly.	◯	◯
The sentences are complete.	◯	◯
The sentences begin with capital letters.	◯	◯
The sentences do not all begin the same way.	◯	◯
The sentences end in periods, question marks, or exclamation points.	◯	◯
Each paragraph talks about only one big idea.	◯	◯
Paragraphs are indented.	◯	◯
Commas are used when needed.	◯	◯
Other punctuation is used correctly.	◯	◯

Building Skills in Writing: Responding to Literature Scholastic Professional Books

Name _____   Date _____

Editing Symbols

Use these symbols when you edit your own writing and your classmates' writing.

Symbol	It Means	Example
≡	Use a capital letter.	Atlanta, georgia
/	Use a lowercase letter.	I like chocolate Ⱡake.
∧	Insert (add) something.	Colin is ᵐʸ brother.
ℓ	Remove something.	It is very very hot.
⊙	Add a period.	The rain fell ⊙
⋏	Add a comma.	I have dogs cats, and fish.
¶	Indent for a new paragraph.	¶ Later that day, Marcie heard a noise.
∿	Transpose (switch position).	Thier house is nearby.

Building Skills in Writing: Responding to Literature   Scholastic Professional Books

Assessing Student Literature Response

Use this Rubric to assess students'
literature-response projects.

RATING SCALE

5 = Beyond expectations   2 = Not quite there
4 = Met expectations   1 = Not there
3 = Almost there   0 = Not applicable to this project

Writing Content							
	Shows evidence that he/she comprehends the literature.	5	4	3	2	1	0
	Advances judgments about the literature.	5	4	3	2	1	0
	Supports judgments with references to the text, other works, other media, or personal knowledge.	5	4	3	2	1	0
	Organizes literature-response writings around main ideas.	5	4	3	2	1	0
	Writes literature-response pieces with attention to purpose and audience.	5	4	3	2	1	0
	Chooses words carefully to express specific ideas.	5	4	3	2	1	0
	Excludes unnecessary and irrelevant information.	5	4	3	2	1	0
	Follows specific project directions.	5	4	3	2	1	0
	Other: _____	5	4	3	2	1	0
Writing Mechanics	Edits work for grammar.	5	4	3	2	1	0
	Edits work for punctuation.	5	4	3	2	1	0
	Edits work for capitalization.	5	4	3	2	1	0
	Spells words correctly.	5	4	3	2	1	0
	Uses clear, complete sentences.	5	4	3	2	1	0
	Indents paragraphs.	5	4	3	2	1	0
	Other: _____	5	4	3	2	1	0

Teacher Rubric